NO READING REQUIRED TO PLAY

I'll tell you what to do!

⭐ **Minimal computer memory required.**

⭐ **Plays on Macs and PCs.**

⭐ **Phonics Fun plays directly from the CD-ROM.**

JUST CLICK THE MOUSE AND GO

No computer skills needed.

Everyone can play.

For ages 2 to 6

 # Follow Puppy to phonics fun!

Bug and Cricket count to two.
Thank you, thank you, that will do.

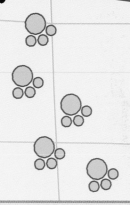

SING AND LEARN SONGS

 Sing along with music videos. Follow the lyrics to learn the words to five favorite songs.

READ THE STORY

When you want to hear a story, click on . Follow along: words light up as they are read.

KEY

 compass   songs   match-a-pair

 read-to-me   look-and-find    pick-a-word

 animation    make-a-picture    puzzles

BUILD VOCABULARY

Click a word and it reads itself. Click a **red** word, and you see and hear a pop-up explanation of how to pronounce that word.

PICK A WORD

Learn to read by matching pictures and words. See fun animations with each correct match.

MATCH THE PAIRS

Develop memory and reading skills by matching objects and words. Each time you play the game is different.

LOOK AND FIND

Build reading skills through rhyming fun. Find and identify up to 30 rhymes and noisy surprises.

SOLVE A PUZZLE

Build visualization and problem-solving skills with seven different puzzles.

MAKE A PICTURE

Use your imagination to make as many pictures as you wish. There are four different backgrounds and lots of characters and objects to click in place. Print the picture when you're finished.

This CD-ROM is easy to use!

Launching the Game

Windows®: Insert the CD-ROM into your CD-ROM drive. AutoRun automatically plays the software. If AutoRun is disabled, double click on the My Computer icon. Then double click on the CD-ROM icon followed by the Start icon.

Macintosh®: Insert the CD-ROM into your CD-ROM drive. AutoRun automatically plays the software. If AutoRun is disabled, double click on the Phonics Fun icon followed by the Start icon.

See Read Me file for helpful hints and other information.

Windows®: To open the Read Me file, double click on the My Computer icon. Right click on the CD-ROM icon and select OPEN. Double click on Readme.htm.

Macintosh®: To open the Read Me file, double click on the Phonics Fun icon. Then double click on the Read Me file.

For support visit our Web site at www.pubint.com.

Made with Macromedia is a trademark of Macromedia, Inc.

Little Explorer
my first interactive storybook

PHONICS FUN

my first interactive storybook

Illustrated by Paul and Alice Sharp

Inked by Brent Cardillo

Publications International, Ltd.

Today is Bug's birthday. Cat makes buns and pancakes for breakfast. "Thank you for the treat," says Bug.

Bug plays with her friends. They go to the park. Bee sees a plane. A friend rides in the plane. Who is it?

Pig was in the plane. He visits Bug for her birthday.

"We will have fun," says Bug.

"Yippee!" say Cat and Bee.

Bug and her friends go to the fair. Pig plays a game. Bee eats lunch. Bug finds three balloons.

Bug and Pig run a race. "Go! Go! Go!" call Bee and Cricket. Bug runs fast. Pig runs slow. Bug wins the race.

After the race they swim in a pool.
The sun is hot. The water is cool.

Bug's friends give her a party. Bug opens presents. Some gifts are big. Some gifts are small. Bug thanks her friends for her presents.

Bug likes music. Her friends like music, too. They play a song together.

Cat reads a book. The story has knights and swords. Cricket and Bee look at the pictures. Pig listens to the words.

s ee

r ead

ch air

st air

bee

bead

Bug rests with her friends. "Birthdays are fun," says Bug. "Thank you for sharing the day with me."